risotto

risotto

30 simply delicious vegetarian
recipes from an Italian kitchen

URSULA FERRIGNO

photography by Jason Lowe

RYLAND
PETERS
& SMALL

LONDON NEW YORK

SENIOR DESIGNER	Ashley Western
COMMISSIONING EDITOR	Elsa Petersen-Schepelern
EDITOR	Maddalena Bastianelli
PRODUCTION	Patricia Harrington
ART DIRECTOR	Gabriella Le Grazie
PUBLISHING DIRECTOR	Alison Starling
FOOD STYLIST	Ursula Ferrigno
COOKING ASSISTANT	Katherine McGhie
STYLIST	Rebecca Duke

AUTHOR'S ACKNOWLEDGMENTS:
A big thank you to Katherine McGhie for her constant support and
assistance, and for being such a perfectionist; and to Kate O'Donnell,
for her utter professionalism and speedy typing. Thanks to the team
at Ryland Peters & Small, especially my editor, Maddie, for her
attention to detail, and for being such fun at the shoots; to Ashley
for designing such a gorgeous book; and to Elsa who invited me to
write it. To Jason, thanks for such beautiful photographs and for all
the laughs we shared. Finally, a special thank you to Antonio
Carluccio for his assistance and generosity with truffles.

NOTES:
Vialone nano is, in my opinion, the best risotto rice. Use this
variety if you can, otherwise use carnaroli or arborio instead.
Please refer to the conversion charts on page 64 if you are used
to working with metric measures.

First published in the United States in 2001
by Ryland Peters & Small, Inc.,
519 Broadway, 5th Floor, New York, NY 10012
www.rylandpeters.com

10 9 8 7 6 5 4 3

Text © Ursula Ferrigno 2001
Design and photographs © Ryland Peters & Small 2001

ISBN 1 84172 147 6

Printed and bound in China

introduction

Italians adore their pasta, but they also love risotto. Throughout Italy, and especially in the north, rice forms a large part of the nation's diet—probably because the dishes are quick to prepare, nutritious, inexpensive, and addictively delicious. They are also very versatile—perfect for relaxed, weekday meals or elegant dinner parties.

Risotto in four easy steps

Top left: Lightly cook shallots in oil and butter until softened.

Top right: Add rice and stir until well coated and glistening.

Bottom left: Add stock, a ladleful at a time, and simmer, stirring until absorbed before adding more. Repeat until all the liquid has been absorbed and the rice is tender but still firm.

Bottom right: Mix in flavorings, such as vegetables, herbs, and cheese.

Risotto is made with short-grain rice, which absorbs a large amount of liquid without the grains losing their bite. There are three main varieties: arborio, carnaroli, and vialone nano. Each one brings a slightly different texture to the dish. Arborio, perhaps the best-known, produces a dense risotto that can become too stiff if overcooked. Carnaroli is the most expensive, but its tender yet firm grain is ideal for risotto. It is also the least likely to overcook. Vialone nano is favored by Venetian cooks and I think it is the best rice. It gives a creamy, voluptuous risotto. Italian delis and an increasing number of supermarkets now sell a good range of risotto rice.

Perfect risotto is easy to achieve. All you need is a good-quality risotto rice, homemade stock, a wide, shallow pan, and 18–20 minutes of constant stirring while the rice cooks. There are no short cuts.

Good risotto is made in stages. The key is to add hot, flavorful stock— a ladleful at a time—to the rice in the pan, stirring constantly until all the liquid has been absorbed and the rice is tender but still firm (*al dente*). It should never be dry or sticky, but have a 'wave-like' (*all'onda*) consistency. A risotto should stand for 2 minutes before serving, then be spooned into warmed bowls, not plates, and served with a fork, never a spoon.

The recipes in this book have been gathered over years of eating out in Italy—many are family recipes given to me by friends. If the vegetables I've suggested are not available, use whatever you can find fresh in the market.

Vegetable Stock

BRODO DI VERDURA

HOMEMADE STOCK (*BRODO*) IS ESSENTIAL WHEN MAKING RISOTTO. IT WILL GIVE THE BEST FLAVOR. MAKE A BASIC STOCK WITH WHATEVER FRESH VEGETABLES ARE AVAILABLE, THEN REFRIGERATE OR FREEZE UNTIL NEEDED.

3 tablespoons unsalted butter
1 tablespoon olive oil
3 garlic cloves, crushed
1 large onion, coarsely chopped
4 leeks, washed and coarsely chopped
2 carrots, coarsely chopped
2 celery stalks, coarsely chopped
1 fennel bulb, coarsely chopped
a handful of fresh flat-leaf parsley, chopped
2 dried bay leaves
2 sprigs of thyme

MAKES ABOUT 4 CUPS

Melt the butter and oil in a large, heavy-bottomed saucepan. Add the garlic, sauté for 2 minutes, then add the remaining ingredients. Cook, stirring constantly, until softened but not browned.

Add 2½ quarts of water and bring to a boil. Reduce the heat, cover, and simmer for 1½ hours. Let cool.

Return the pan to the heat and simmer for 15 minutes. Strain the stock and return to the pan. Discard the solids. Boil rapidly until reduced by half, then use as needed or let cool and keep in the refrigerator for up to 3 days.

FONTINA, GORGONZOLA, TALEGGIO, AND PARMESAN ARE MY FAVORITE FOUR CHEESES. TRY

MIXING AND MATCHING YOUR OWN SELECTION OF CHEESES, BUT CHOOSE ONES THAT ARE QUITE

CREAMY AND HAVE A GOOD FLAVOR. USE THEM AT ROOM TEMPERATURE FOR MAXIMUM TASTE.

Risotto with Four Cheeses
RISOTTO AI QUATTRO FORMAGGI

Put the stock in a saucepan. Heat until almost boiling, then reduce the heat until barely simmering to keep it hot.

Heat the butter and oil in a deep skillet or heavy-bottomed saucepan over a medium heat. Add the shallots and cook for 1–2 minutes, until softened but not browned. Add the garlic.

Add the rice and stir with a wooden spoon until the grains are well coated and glistening, about 1 minute. Pour in the wine and stir until it has been completely absorbed.

Add 1 ladle of hot stock and simmer, stirring until it has been absorbed. Continue to add the stock at intervals and cook as before, until the liquid has been absorbed and the rice is tender but still firm (*al dente*), about 18–20 minutes. Reserve the last ladle of stock.

Add the reserved stock, the four cheeses, parsley, salt, and pepper. Mix well. Remove from the heat, cover, and let rest for 2 minutes.

Spoon into warmed bowls, sprinkle with grated Parmesan, and serve.

4 cups vegetable stock (page 8)
¼ cup unsalted butter
1 tablespoon olive oil
8 shallots, finely chopped
1 garlic clove, crushed
1½ cups risotto rice, such as
    vialone nano, carnaroli, or arborio
½ cup white wine
1½ cups freshly grated Parmesan cheese,
    plus extra to serve
2 oz. Gorgonzola cheese, cut into cubes
2 oz. Fontina cheese, cut into cubes
2 oz. Taleggio cheese, rind removed and
    cheese cut into cubes
a handful of fresh flat-leaf parsley,
    coarsely chopped
sea salt and freshly ground black pepper

SERVES 4

Risotto with Watercress and Taleggio

RISOTTO AL CRESCIONE E TALEGGIO

TALEGGIO—NAMED AFTER A VALLEY IN BERGAMO WHERE IT ORIGINATES—IS MADE FROM THE MILK OF COWS THAT GRAZE THE ALPINE PASTURES, THEN THE CHEESE IS RIPENED IN CAVES. ITS SWEET FLAVOR COMPLEMENTS THE PEPPERY TASTE OF WATERCRESS. ARUGULA WITH TALEGGIO IS ALSO DELICIOUS.

Put the stock in a saucepan. Heat until almost boiling, then reduce the heat until barely simmering to keep it hot.

Heat 2 tablespoons of the butter and the oil in a deep skillet or heavy-bottomed saucepan over a medium heat. Add the shallots and cook for 1–2 minutes, until softened but not browned.

Add the rice and stir with a wooden spoon until the grains are well coated and glistening, about 1 minute. Pour in the wine and stir until it has been completely absorbed.

Add 1 ladle of hot stock and simmer, stirring until it has been absorbed. Repeat. After 10 minutes, add the watercress and mix well. Continue to add the stock at intervals and cook as before, for 8–10 minutes longer, until the liquid has been absorbed and the rice is tender but still firm (*al dente*).

Mix in the Parmesan, Taleggio, the remaining butter, salt, and pepper. Remove from the heat, cover, and let rest for 2 minutes.

Spoon into warmed bowls, top with watercress leaves, and serve.

4 cups vegetable stock (page 8)
1/3 cup unsalted butter
1 tablespoon olive oil
8 shallots, finely chopped
1½ cups risotto rice, such as vialone nano, carnaroli, or arborio
1/3 cup white wine
a bunch of watercress, trimmed and chopped, plus extra leaves to serve
1½ cups freshly grated Parmesan cheese
7 oz. Taleggio cheese, rind removed and cheese cut into cubes
sea salt and freshly ground black pepper

SERVES 4

Arugula and Blue Cheese Risotto

RISOTTO CON ARUGULA E GORGONZOLA

AGED GORGONZOLA (PICCANTE) IS A HIGHLY AROMATIC AND PUNGENT BLUE-VEINED CHEESE.

IF THE FLAVOR IS TOO STRONG FOR YOUR LIKING, REPLACE IT WITH DOLCELATTE—A YOUNGER, MILDER

VERSION. GORGONZOLA IS QUITE SALTY, SO TASTE THE RISOTTO FIRST AND ADD SALT IF NECESSARY.

Put the stock in a saucepan. Heat until almost boiling, then reduce the heat until barely simmering to keep it hot.

Heat the butter and oil in a deep skillet or heavy-bottomed saucepan over a medium heat. Add the shallots and cook for 1–2 minutes, until softened but not browned. Add the garlic.

Add the rice and stir with a wooden spoon until the grains are well coated and glistening, about 1 minute.

Add 1 ladle of hot stock and simmer, stirring until it has been absorbed. Continue to add the stock at intervals and cook as before, until the liquid has been absorbed and the rice is tender but still firm (*al dente*), about 18–20 minutes.

Mix in the arugula, Parmesan, Gorgonzola, salt, and pepper. Remove from the heat, cover, and let rest for 2 minutes.

Spoon into warmed bowls, drizzle with extra virgin olive oil, if using, and serve immediately.

4 cups vegetable stock (page 8)
¼ cup unsalted butter
1 tablespoon olive oil
8 shallots, finely chopped
2 garlic cloves, crushed
1½ cups risotto rice, such as vialone nano, carnaroli, or arborio
2 large handfuls of arugula leaves
1½ cups freshly grated Parmesan cheese
2 oz. Gorgonzola piccante cheese, cut into cubes
sea salt and freshly ground black pepper
extra virgin olive oil, to serve (optional)

SERVES 4

Saffron Risotto

RISOTTO ALLA MILANESE

THIS CLASSIC RISOTTO IS A SPECIALTY OF LOMBARDY. USE SAFFRON STRANDS RATHER THAN THE POWDERED FORM, WHICH TENDS TO BE OF A LESSER QUALITY AND FLAVOR. MY SISTERS MAKE THIS DISH OFTEN FOR THEIR FAMILIES AND IT IS PARTICULARLY POPULAR WITH THE CHILDREN.

Put the stock in a saucepan. Heat until almost boiling, then reduce the heat until barely simmering to keep it hot.

Heat the butter and oil in a deep skillet or heavy-bottomed saucepan over a medium heat. Add the shallots and cook for 1–2 minutes, until softened but not browned. Add the saffron and stir until the yellow color is released.

Add the rice and stir with a wooden spoon until the grains are well coated and glistening, about 1 minute. Pour in the wine and stir until it has been completely absorbed.

Add 1 ladle of hot stock and simmer, stirring until it has been absorbed. Continue to add the stock at intervals and cook as before, until the liquid has been absorbed and the rice is tender but still firm (al dente), about 18–20 minutes. Reserve the last ladle of stock.

Add the reserved stock, Parmesan, cream, parsley, if using, salt, and pepper. Mix well. Remove from the heat, cover, and let rest for 2 minutes.

Spoon into warmed bowls and serve immediately.

4 cups vegetable stock (page 8)
¼ cup unsalted butter
1 tablespoon olive oil
8 shallots, finely chopped
½ teaspoon saffron strands
1½ cups risotto rice, such as vialone nano, carnaroli, or arborio
⅓ cup white wine
1½ cups freshly grated Parmesan cheese
2 tablespoons light cream
a handful of fresh flat-leaf parsley, coarsely chopped (optional)
sea salt and freshly ground black pepper

SERVES 4

Risotto with Zucchini and Ricotta
RISOTTO CON ZUCCHINE E RICOTTA

WONDERFUL PRODUCE FROM A LOCAL MARKET IN UMBRIA INSPIRED THIS CREAMY RISOTTO. SMALL, GARDEN-FRESH ZUCCHINI AND MILKY WHITE, FLUFFY RICOTTA ARE ESSENTIAL. ITALIAN STORES AND SOME SUPERMARKETS SELL FRESH RICOTTA.

½ cup unsalted butter
4 small zucchini, about 7 oz., diced
a handful of fresh mint, leaves torn
a handful of fresh flat-leaf parsley,
  coarsely chopped
4 cups vegetable stock (page 8)
1 tablespoon olive oil
8 shallots, finely chopped
2 garlic cloves, crushed
1½ cups risotto rice, such as vialone nano,
  carnaroli, or arborio
½ cup white wine
⅓ cup fresh ricotta cheese
1½ cups freshly grated Parmesan cheese
sea salt and freshly ground black pepper

SERVES 4

Melt half the butter in a skillet, add the zucchini, and cook over medium heat until tender, about 5 minutes. Add the mint and parsley and mix well. Set aside.

Put the stock in a saucepan. Heat until almost boiling, then reduce the heat until barely simmering to keep it hot.

Heat the remaining butter and the oil in a deep skillet or heavy-bottomed saucepan over a medium heat. Add the shallots and cook for 1–2 minutes, until softened but not browned. Add the garlic and mix well.

Add the rice and stir with a wooden spoon until the grains are well coated and glistening, about 1 minute. Pour in the wine and stir until it has been completely absorbed.

Add 1 ladle of hot stock and simmer, stirring until the liquid has been absorbed. Continue to add the stock at intervals and cook as before, until all the liquid has been absorbed and the rice is tender but still firm (*al dente*), about 18–20 minutes.

Add the cooked zucchini, ricotta, Parmesan, salt, and pepper. Mix well. Remove from the heat, cover, and let rest for 2 minutes.

Spoon into warmed bowls and serve immediately.

Barolo Risotto

RISOTTO AL BAROLO

RED WINE RISOTTO IS TRADITIONAL IN MANY GRAPE-GROWING REGIONS IN ITALY. THIS ONE IN PARTICULAR IS FAMOUS. IT IS A SPECIALITY OF PIEDMONT AND IS MADE WITH THE LOCAL BAROLO. IF THIS WINE IS NOT AVAILABLE, CHOOSE ONE THAT IS FULL-BODIED WITH ROBUST, FRUITY FLAVORS.

Put the stock in a saucepan. Heat until almost boiling, then reduce the heat until barely simmering to keep it hot.

Heat half the butter and the oil in a deep skillet or heavy-bottomed saucepan over a medium heat. Add the shallots, carrot, and celery and cook for 1–2 minutes, until softened but not browned. Add the garlic and mix well.

Add the rice and stir with a wooden spoon until the grains are well coated and glistening, about 1 minute. Pour in half the wine and stir until it has been completely absorbed.

Add 1 ladle of hot stock and simmer, stirring until it has been absorbed. Continue to add the stock at intervals and cook as before, until all the liquid has been absorbed and the rice is tender but still firm (*al dente*), about 18–20 minutes.

Add the remaining wine and butter, the Parmesan and parsley, salt, and pepper. Mix well. Remove from the heat, cover, and let rest for 2 minutes.

Spoon into warmed bowls and serve immediately.

4 cups vegetable stock (page 8)
½ cup unsalted butter
1 tablespoon olive oil
8 shallots, finely chopped
1 carrot, finely chopped
2 celery stalks, finely chopped
1 garlic clove, crushed
1½ cups risotto rice, such as vialone nano, carnaroli, or arborio
2 cups Barolo wine or full-bodied red wine
1½ cups freshly grated Parmesan cheese
a handful of fresh flat-leaf parsley, coarsely chopped
sea salt and freshly ground black pepper

SERVES 4

Rice Balls

SUPPLÌ DI RISO

THESE CHEESE-RICE BALLS, ALSO KNOWN AS *SUPPLÌ AL TELEFONO*, ARE ENJOYED THROUGHOUT ITALY. IN SICILY THEY ARE CALLED *ARANCINI*, MEANING LITTLE ORANGES. THIS IS A GOOD WAY OF USING RISOTTO TO MAKE DELICIOUS PARTY FOOD OR ANTIPASTO. IT'S FUN TOO.

3½ cups vegetable stock (page 8)
¼ cup unsalted butter
1½ cups risotto rice, such as vialone nano,
    carnaroli, or arborio
6 oz. mozzarella cheese, cut into small cubes
6 shallots, finely chopped
a handful of mixed fresh herbs, such as
    parsley, basil, and oregano, chopped
finely grated zest of 1 large orange
½ cup freshly grated Parmesan cheese
⅓ cup olive oil, for sautéing
sea salt and freshly ground black pepper

BREADCRUMB COATING:
1 egg, lightly beaten
1 cup fresh breadcrumbs

MAKES 8, SERVES 4

Put the stock in a saucepan. Heat until almost boiling, then reduce the heat until barely simmering to keep it hot.

Melt the butter in a wide saucepan. Add the rice and stir with a wooden spoon until the grains are well coated and glistening, about 1 minute. Add 1 ladle of hot stock and simmer, stirring until it has been absorbed. Continue to add the stock at intervals and cook as before, until all the liquid has been absorbed and the rice is tender but still firm (*al dente*), about 18–20 minutes.

Add the mozzarella, shallots, mixed herbs, orange zest, Parmesan, salt, and pepper. Mix well. Remove from the heat and let cool. The rice is easier to handle and shape when it is cold.

Using your hands, shape the flavored rice into 8 balls. Dip each one into the beaten egg and coat well, then roll them in the breadcrumbs, pressing crumbs onto any uncovered area.

Heat the oil in a skillet, add the rice balls (in batches, if necessary), and cook until golden on all sides, about 8 minutes. Drain well on paper towels. Serve hot or cold.

Fontina and Walnut Risotto

RISOTTO CON FONTINA E NOCI

FONTINA IS A MOUNTAIN CHEESE FROM LOMBARDY AND IT IS DELICATELY FLAVORED—MILD ENOUGH NOT TO OVERPOWER THE WALNUTS. I FIRST HAD THIS COMFORTING RISOTTO ON A COLD BUT BRIGHT WINTRY DAY IN BERGAMO, IN THE NORTH OF ITALY. FONTINA IS ALSO USED IN LASAGNE, *FONDUTA*—A KIND OF FONDUE—OR, AS I LIKE IT, MELTED IN A TOASTED SANDWICH FILLED WITH ARUGULA.

4 cups vegetable stock (page 8)
¼ cup unsalted butter
1 tablespoon olive oil
8 shallots, finely chopped
1 garlic clove, crushed
1½ cups risotto rice, such as
    vialone nano, carnaroli, or arborio
⅓ cup white wine
4 oz. Fontina cheese, cut into cubes
1½ cups freshly grated Parmesan cheese
⅓ cup walnut pieces, coarsely chopped
a handful of fresh flat-leaf parsley,
    coarsely chopped
sea salt and freshly ground black pepper

TO SERVE (OPTIONAL):
walnut pieces, coarsely chopped
freshly grated Parmesan cheese

SERVES 4

Put the stock in a saucepan. Heat until almost boiling, then reduce the heat until barely simmering to keep it hot.

Heat the butter and oil in a deep skillet or heavy-bottomed saucepan over a medium heat. Add the shallots and cook for 1–2 minutes, until softened but not browned. Add the garlic.

Add the rice and stir with a wooden spoon until the grains are well coated and glistening, about 1 minute. Pour in the wine and stir until it has been completely absorbed.

Add 1 ladle of hot stock and simmer, stirring until it has been absorbed. Continue to add the stock at intervals and cook as before, until the liquid has been absorbed and the rice is tender but still firm (*al dente*), about 18–20 minutes. Reserve the last ladle of stock.

Add the reserved stock, Fontina, Parmesan, walnuts, parsley, salt, and pepper. Stir well. Remove from the heat, cover, and let rest for 2 minutes.

Spoon into warmed bowls, sprinkle with walnuts and grated Parmesan, if using, and serve immediately.

Potato, Basil, and Green Bean Risotto

RISOTTO ALLA GENOVESE

A CLASSIC RISOTTO FROM GENOA. AT FIRST YOU MIGHT BE ALARMED AT THE COMBINATION OF POTATOES, RICE, AND BEANS. DON'T BE, IT'S ABSOLUTELY DELICIOUS AND MAKES A SUBSTANTIAL MEAL. SPOONING FRESH PESTO (HOMEMADE OR STORE-BOUGHT) ON TOP BEFORE SERVING IS OPTIONAL, BUT IF YOU LOVE BASIL, THIS WILL INTENSIFY THE FLAVOR DRAMATICALLY.

Put the stock in a saucepan. Heat until almost boiling, then reduce the heat until barely simmering to keep it hot.

Heat the butter and oil in a deep skillet or heavy-bottomed saucepan over a medium heat. Add the shallots and cook for 1–2 minutes, until softened but not browned. Add the garlic.

Add the rice and stir with a wooden spoon until the grains are well coated and glistening, about 1 minute. Pour in the wine and stir until it has been completely absorbed.

Add the potatoes and beans. Add 1 ladle of hot stock and simmer, stirring until it has been absorbed. Continue to add the stock at intervals and cook as before, until all the liquid has been absorbed and the rice is tender but still firm (*al dente*), about 18–20 minutes.

Add the Parmesan, basil, salt, and pepper. Mix well. Remove from the heat, cover, and let rest for 2 minutes.

Spoon into warmed bowls, top with basil, and drizzle with olive oil or fresh pesto, if using. Serve immediately.

4 cups vegetable stock (page 8)
¼ cup unsalted butter
1 tablespoon olive oil
8 shallots, finely chopped
2 garlic cloves, crushed
1½ cups risotto rice, such as vialone nano, carnaroli, or arborio
⅓ cup white wine
12 new potatoes, scrubbed and cut into halves or quarters
2 oz. green beans, cut into ½-inch lengths, about ½ cup
1½ cups freshly grated Parmesan cheese
a large handful of fresh basil, leaves torn
sea salt and freshly ground black pepper

TO SERVE:
fresh basil leaves
olive oil (optional)
fresh pesto (optional)

SERVES 4

Risotto with Chickpeas and Tomatoes
RISOTTO CON CECI E POMODORI

CHICKPEAS ARE A FAVORITE IN ITALIAN COOKING, ADDED TO SOUPS, PASTA, RICE, AND SALADS. THEY HAVE A NUTTY FLAVOR, CREAMY TEXTURE, AND ARE PACKED WITH ENERGY.

Put the stock in a saucepan. Bring to a boil, then reduce the heat until barely simmering to keep it hot.

Heat the butter and oil in a deep skillet or heavy-bottomed saucepan over a medium heat. Add the shallots and cook for 1–2 minutes, until softened but not browned. Add the garlic.

Add the rice and stir with a wooden spoon until the grains are well coated and glistening, about 1 minute. Pour in the wine and stir until it has been completely absorbed.

Add 1 ladle of hot stock and simmer, stirring until it has been absorbed. Continue to add the stock at intervals and cook as before, until the liquid has been absorbed and the rice is tender but still firm (*al dente*), about 18–20 minutes. Reserve the last ladle of stock.

Add the reserved stock, chickpeas, tomatoes, Parmesan, parsley, salt, and pepper. Mix well. Remove from the heat, cover, and let rest for 2 minutes.

Spoon into warmed bowls and serve immediately.

4 cups vegetable stock (page 8)
¼ cup unsalted butter
1 tablespoon olive oil
8 shallots, finely chopped
2 garlic cloves, crushed
1½ cups risotto rice, such as vialone nano, carnaroli, or arborio
⅓ cup white wine
½ cup cooked chickpeas or canned, rinsed and drained
4–6 medium Italian plum tomatoes, seeded and chopped
1½ cups freshly grated Parmesan cheese
a handful of fresh flat-leaf parsley, coarsely chopped
sea salt and freshly ground black pepper

SERVES 4

Risotto with **Beans**

RISOTTO CON FAGIOLI

BEANS WITH PASTA OR RICE MAKE A MUCH-LOVED MEAL IN ITALY. CANNELLINI BEANS (WHITE KIDNEY BEANS) ARE BEST, BUT NAVY OR GREAT NORTHERN BEANS WORK TOO. USE CARNAROLI IN THIS DISH; IT HAS LESS STARCH THAN OTHER RISOTTO RICE AND ITS TEXTURE EQUALS THAT OF THE BEANS.

4 cups vegetable stock (page 8)
¼ cup unsalted butter
2 tablespoons olive oil
8 shallots, finely chopped
2 garlic cloves, crushed
1½ cups carnaroli rice
⅓ cup white wine
1¼ cups cooked cannellini beans or canned, rinsed and drained
4 medium Italian plum tomatoes, seeded and chopped
grated zest of 1 lemon
1½ cups freshly grated Parmesan cheese
a handful of freshly torn basil or finely chopped rosemary
a handful of fresh flat-leaf parsley, finely chopped
sea salt and freshly ground black pepper
extra virgin olive oil, to serve (optional)

SERVES 4

Put the stock in a saucepan. Heat until almost boiling, then reduce the heat until barely simmering to keep it hot.

Heat the butter and 1 tablespoon of the oil in a deep skillet or heavy-bottomed saucepan over a medium heat. Add the shallots and cook for 1–2 minutes, until softened but not browned. Add the garlic and mix well.

Add the rice and stir with a wooden spoon until the grains are well coated and glistening, about 1 minute. Pour in the wine and stir until it has been completely absorbed.

Add 1 ladle of hot stock and simmer, stirring until it has been absorbed. After 10 minutes, add the cannellini beans, tomatoes, and lemon zest and mix well. Continue to add the stock at intervals and cook as before, for a further 8–10 minutes, until the liquid has been absorbed and the rice is tender but still firm (*al dente*).

Add the Parmesan, half the herbs, salt, and pepper. Stir well. Remove from the heat, cover, and let rest for 2 minutes.

Spoon into warmed bowls, sprinkle with the remaining herbs, and drizzle with extra virgin olive oil, if using. Serve immediately.

Fava Bean and Red Onion Risotto
RISOTTO CON FAVE E CIPOLLA ROSSA

FAVA BEANS ARE AT THEIR MOST TENDER WHEN YOUNG AND SMALL. ONCE SHELLED, THEY NEED NO OTHER PREPARATION. ONLY LARGER, OLDER BEANS NEED TO BE BLANCHED FIRST, THEN POPPED OUT OF THEIR TOUGH, GRAY OUTER CASING. LIMA BEANS MAKE A GOOD ALTERNATIVE FOR THIS DISH.

4 cups vegetable stock (see page 8)
¼ cup unsalted butter
1 tablespoon olive oil
8 shallots, finely chopped
2 garlic cloves, crushed
1½ cups risotto rice, such as vialone nano, carnaroli, or arborio
½ cup white wine
2 red onions, finely chopped
2 cups fresh or frozen shelled fava beans
1½ cups freshly grated Parmesan cheese
a handful of fresh mint, chopped
sea salt and freshly ground black pepper

SERVES 4

Put the stock in a saucepan. Heat until almost boiling, then reduce the heat until barely simmering to keep it hot.

Heat the butter and oil in a deep skillet or heavy-bottomed saucepan over a medium heat. Add the shallots and cook for 1–2 minutes, until softened but not browned. Add the garlic.

Add the rice and stir with a wooden spoon until the grains are well coated and glistening, about 1 minute. Pour in the wine and stir until it has been completely absorbed.

Add 1 ladle of hot stock and simmer, stirring until it has been absorbed. Repeat. After 10 minutes, add the onions and fava beans. Continue to add the stock at intervals and cook as before, until the liquid has been absorbed and the rice is tender but still firm (*al dente*), about 18–20 minutes. Reserve the last ladle of stock.

Add the reserved stock, Parmesan, mint, salt, and pepper. Mix well. Remove from the heat, cover, and let rest for 2 minutes.

Spoon into warmed bowls and serve immediately.

Risotto with Asparagus, Peas, and Basil

RISOTTO CON ASPARAGI, PISELLI, E BASILICO

ONE OF MY ALL-TIME FAVORITE RISOTTOS—SO LIGHT, FRESH, AND VIBRANTLY GREEN. IT REMINDS ME OF EARLY SUMMER, WHEN ASPARAGUS AND PEAS GROW IN ABUNDANCE. TRY TO USE VEGETABLES WHEN THEY ARE IN SEASON, SO THAT YOU CAN ENJOY THEM AT THEIR FINEST AND SWEETEST.

4 cups vegetable stock (page 8)
¼ cup unsalted butter
1 tablespoon olive oil
8 shallots, finely chopped
1½ cups risotto rice, such as vialone nano, carnaroli, or arborio
⅓ cup white wine
12 oz. asparagus, trimmed and cut into 2-inch lengths
1 cup fresh or frozen shelled peas
finely grated zest of 1 lemon
1½ cups freshly grated Parmesan cheese
a large handful of fresh basil, leaves torn
sea salt and freshly ground black pepper

TO SERVE (OPTIONAL):
fresh basil leaves
freshly grated Parmesan cheese

SERVES 4

Put the stock in a saucepan. Heat until almost boiling, then reduce the heat until barely simmering to keep it hot.

Heat the butter and oil in a deep skillet or heavy-bottomed saucepan over a medium heat. Add the shallots and cook for 1–2 minutes, until softened but not browned.

Add the rice and stir with a wooden spoon until the grains are well coated and glistening, about 1 minute. Pour in the wine and stir until it has been completely absorbed.

Add 1 ladle of hot stock and simmer, stirring until it has been absorbed. Repeat. After 10 minutes, add the asparagus, peas, and lemon zest and mix well. Continue to add the stock at intervals and cook as before, for a further 8–10 minutes, until the liquid has been absorbed and the rice is tender but still firm (*al dente*).

Add the reserved stock, Parmesan, basil, salt, and pepper. Mix well. Remove from the heat, cover, and let rest for 2 minutes.

Spoon into warmed bowls and top with basil and grated Parmesan, if using. Serve immediately.

VEGETABLES

Mushroom Risotto with Potatoes

RISOTTO AI FUNGHI CON PATATE

MUSHROOM RISOTTO IS ALWAYS POPULAR. PORTOBELLO MUSHROOMS HAVE AN INTENSE FLAVOR, BUT YOU CAN USE WHATEVER KIND YOU LIKE. FOR A SPECIAL TREAT, USE WILD MUSHROOMS, SUCH AS PORCINI AND CHANTERELLES. I'VE ADDED POTATOES FOR EXTRA FLAVOR AND TEXTURE.

4 cups vegetable stock (page 8)
¼ cup unsalted butter
1 tablespoon olive oil
8 shallots, finely chopped
2 garlic cloves crushed
8 oz. portobello mushrooms or mixed wild
   mushrooms, cut into chunks if large
4 medium new potatoes, scrubbed and cut
   into small chunks
1 sprig of rosemary, finely chopped
1½ cups risotto rice, such as vialone nano,
   carnaroli, or arborio
⅓ cup white wine
1½ cups freshly grated Parmesan cheese
2 tablespoons light cream
a handful of fresh flat-leaf parsley,
   coarsely chopped, plus extra to serve
sea salt and freshly ground black pepper

SERVES 4

Put the stock in a saucepan. Heat until almost boiling, then reduce the heat until barely simmering to keep it hot.

Heat the butter and oil in a deep skillet or heavy-bottomed saucepan over a medium heat. Add the shallots and cook for 1–2 minutes, until softened but not browned. Add the garlic, mushrooms, potatoes, and rosemary. Mix well.

Add the rice and stir with a wooden spoon until the grains are well coated and glistening, about 1 minute. Pour in the wine and stir until it has been completely absorbed.

Add 1 ladle of hot stock and simmer, stirring until it has been absorbed. Continue to add the stock at intervals and cook as before, until the liquid has been absorbed and the rice is tender but still firm (*al dente*), about 18–20 minutes. Reserve the last ladle of stock.

Add the reserved stock, Parmesan, cream, parsley, salt, and pepper. Mix well. Remove from the heat, cover, and let rest for 2 minutes.

Spoon into warmed bowls, sprinkle with chopped parsley, and serve immediately.

Pumpkin Risotto

RISOTTO DI ZUCCA

A GREAT FAVORITE IN NORTHERN ITALY. I ADORE PUMPKIN AND IN ITALY IT IS EATEN ALL YEAR ROUND, NOT JUST IN THE FALL. IT IS USED IN ENDLESS WAYS—SWEET AND SAVORY—FROM SOUPS TO STEWS AND FROM PASTA FILLINGS TO FLAVORED BREADS AND CAKES. PUMPKINS VARY ENORMOUSLY—THE BEST ONES TO USE ARE THE SMALLER PIE PUMPKINS.

Put the stock in a saucepan. Heat until almost boiling, then reduce the heat until barely simmering to keep it hot.

Heat the butter and oil in a deep skillet or heavy-bottomed saucepan over a medium heat. Add the shallots and cook for 1–2 minutes, until softened but not browned. Add the garlic.

Add the rice and stir with a wooden spoon until the grains are well coated and glistening, about 1 minute. Pour in the wine and stir until it has been completely absorbed.

Add 1 ladle of hot stock, the pumpkin or butternut and parsley. Simmer, stirring until the liquid has been absorbed. Continue to add the stock at intervals and cook as before, until the liquid has been absorbed, the pumpkin is cooked, and the rice is tender but firm (*al dente*), about 18–20 minutes. Reserve the last ladle of stock.

Add the reserved stock, Parmesan, salt, and pepper. Mix well. Remove from the heat, cover, and let rest for 2 minutes.

Spoon into warmed bowls and serve immediately.

4 cups vegetable stock (page 8)
¼ cup unsalted butter
1 tablespoon olive oil
8 shallots, finely chopped
2 garlic cloves, crushed
1½ cups risotto rice, such as vialone nano, carnaroli, or arborio
½ cup white wine
2 cups diced pumpkin or butternut squash
a handful of fresh flat-leaf parsley, coarsely chopped
1½ cups freshly grated Parmesan cheese
sea salt and freshly ground black pepper

SERVES 4

Tomato Risotto

RISOTTO AL POMODORO

I LIKE THE SIMPLICITY OF THIS DISH—THIS IS PROBABLY WHY IT'S POPULAR WITH CHILDREN AS WELL AS GROWN-UPS. IT'S ALMOST IMPOSSIBLE TO IMAGINE ITALIAN FOOD WITHOUT TOMATOES—USE SUN-RIPENED TOMATOES THAT ARE FIRM, RED, AND WITH A GOOD FRUITY SCENT.

4 cups vegetable stock (page 8)
¼ cup unsalted butter
1 tablespoon olive oil
8 shallots, finely chopped
2 garlic cloves, crushed
1½ cups risotto rice, such as vialone nano, carnaroli, or arborio
⅓ cup white wine
8 firm tomatoes, seeded and coarsely chopped
1½ cups freshly grated Parmesan cheese, plus extra to serve
a large handful of fresh basil, leaves torn
sea salt and freshly ground black pepper

SERVES 4

Put the stock in a saucepan. Heat until almost boiling, then reduce the heat until barely simmering to keep it hot.

Heat the butter and oil in a deep skillet or heavy-bottomed saucepan over a medium heat. Add the shallots and cook for 1–2 minutes, until softened but not browned. Add the garlic.

Add the rice and stir with a wooden spoon until the grains are well coated and glistening, about 1 minute. Pour in the wine and stir until it has been completely absorbed.

Add 1 ladle of hot stock and simmer, stirring until it has been absorbed. Repeat. After 10 minutes, add the tomatoes. Continue to add the stock at intervals and cook as before, for a further 8–10 minutes, until the liquid has been absorbed and the tomatoes and rice are tender but still firm (*al dente*). Reserve the last ladle of stock.

Add the reserved stock, Parmesan, basil, salt, and pepper. Mix well. Remove from the heat, cover, and let rest for 2 minutes.

Spoon into warmed bowls, sprinkle with grated Parmesan, and serve immediately.

Radicchio Risotto

RISOTTO AL RADICCHIO

MADDALENA CHEPELLO—A FAMILY FRIEND—TAUGHT ME HOW TO COOK THIS COLORFUL VEGETABLE.

THERE ARE TWO VARIETIES; ROUND AND LONG (TREVISO). USE TREVISO, IF YOU CAN—IT IS LESS BITTER

AND HAS MORE FLAVOR. MY FATHER GROWS RADICCHIO, SO I HAVE A SPECIAL FONDNESS FOR IT.

4 cups vegetable stock (page 8)
¼ cup unsalted butter
1 tablespoon olive oil
8 shallots, finely chopped
1½ cups risotto rice, such as vialone nano,
    carnaroli, or arborio
⅓ cup white wine
2 medium radicchio, preferably Treviso,
    finely sliced
1½ cups freshly grated Parmesan cheese, plus
    extra to serve
2 tablespoons light cream
a handful of fresh basil, leaves torn
sea salt and freshly ground black pepper

SERVES 4

Put the stock in a saucepan. Heat until almost boiling, then reduce the heat until barely simmering to keep it hot.

Heat the butter and oil in a deep skillet or heavy-bottomed saucepan over a medium heat. Add the shallots and cook for 1–2 minutes, until softened but not browned.

Add the rice and stir with a wooden spoon until the grains are well coated and glistening, about 1 minute. Pour in the wine and stir until it has been completely absorbed.

Add 1 ladle of hot stock and simmer, stirring until it has been absorbed. Repeat. After 10 minutes, add the radicchio. Continue to add the stock at intervals and cook as before, for a further 8–10 minutes, until the liquid has been absorbed and the rice is tender but still firm (al dente). Reserve the last ladle of stock.

Add the reserved stock, Parmesan, cream, basil, salt, and pepper. Mix well. Remove from the heat, cover, and let rest for 2 minutes.

Spoon into warmed bowls, sprinkle with grated Parmesan and serve.

Risotto with Sage and Leeks

RISOTTO CON SALVIA E PORRI

SAGE IS A PUNGENT HERB, SAID TO HAVE MEMORY-ENHANCING PROPERTIES. ADD LESS SAGE IF YOU FIND IT TOO OVERPOWERING. YOUNG AND TENDER LEEKS HAVE THE MOST FLAVOR—WASH THEM WELL TO GET RID OF ANY SOIL TRAPPED BETWEEN THE TIGHTLY PACKED LEAVES.

4 cups vegetable stock (page 8)
¼ cup unsalted butter
1 tablespoon olive oil
8 shallots, finely chopped
a handful of fresh sage, finely chopped
1 garlic clove, crushed
1½ cups risotto rice, such as vialone nano,
   carnaroli, or arborio
⅓ cup white wine
6 baby leeks, washed and finely chopped*
1½ cups freshly grated Parmesan cheese
2 tablespoons light cream
sea salt and freshly ground black pepper
4 sage leaves, to serve

SERVES 4

Put the stock in a saucepan. Heat until almost boiling, then reduce the heat until barely simmering to keep it hot.

Heat the butter and oil in a deep skillet or heavy-bottomed saucepan over a medium heat. Add the shallots and sage and cook for 2–3 minutes, until softened and lightly golden. Add the garlic.

Add the rice and stir with a wooden spoon until the grains are well coated and glistening, about 1 minute. Pour in the wine, stir until it has been completely absorbed, then add the leeks. Mix well.

Add 1 ladle of hot stock and simmer, stirring until it has been absorbed. Continue to add the stock at intervals and cook as before, until the liquid has been absorbed and the rice is tender but still firm (al dente), about 18–20 minutes. Reserve the last ladle of stock.

Add the reserved stock, Parmesan, cream, salt, and pepper. Mix well. Remove from the heat, cover, and let rest for 2 minutes.

Spoon into warmed bowls, top with a sage leaf, and serve.

*Note: To clean leeks, cut them in half or quarters down the middle and rinse, shaking them under running water, to dislodge any trapped dirt.

Fennel Risotto

RISOTTO AL FINOCCHIO

WE ITALIANS LOVE FENNEL AND EAT IT BOTH RAW AND COOKED. IT HAS A DISTINCTIVE, ANISEED-LIKE FLAVOR. TO CLEANSE THE PALATE AFTER A LARGE MEAL, WE EAT IT RAW AS A DIGESTIVE, SO WE CAN CONTINUE TO EAT EVEN MORE. TRY IT—IT WORKS.

Wash and trim the fennel, removing all the hard external green bits. Cut off and reserve the green fronds. Finely slice the fennel.

Put the stock in a saucepan. Heat until almost boiling, then reduce the heat until barely simmering to keep it hot.

Heat the butter and oil in a deep skillet or heavy-bottomed saucepan over a medium heat. Add the shallots and cook for 1–2 minutes, until softened but not browned. Add the fennel and lemon zest and mix well.

Add the rice and stir with a wooden spoon until the grains are well coated and glistening, about 1 minute. Pour in the wine and stir until it has been completely absorbed.

Add 1 ladle of hot stock and simmer, stirring until it has been absorbed. Continue to add the stock at intervals and cook as before, until the liquid has been absorbed and the rice is tender but still firm (al dente), about 18–20 minutes. Reserve the last ladle of stock.

Add the reserved stock, Parmesan, cream, salt, and pepper. Mix well. Remove from the heat, cover, and let rest for 2 minutes.

Spoon into warmed bowls, top with the reserved fennel fronds, and serve.

2 medium fennel bulbs with green fronds
4 cups vegetable stock (page 8)
¼ cup unsalted butter
1 tablespoon olive oil
8 shallots, finely chopped
finely grated zest of 2 lemons
1½ cups risotto rice, such as vialone nano, carnaroli, or arborio
⅓ cup white wine
1½ cups freshly grated Parmesan cheese
2 tablespoons light cream
sea salt and freshly ground black pepper

SERVES 4

Chestnut Risotto

RISOTTO DI CASTAGNE

IN ITALY, THE SEASON FOR CHESTNUTS IS VERY SHORT: FROM THE BEGINNING OF NOVEMBER TO MID DECEMBER. FRESH CHESTNUTS HAVE A WONDERFUL NUTTY FLAVOR, BUT IF THEY'RE NOT IN SEASON OR YOU DON'T HAVE TIME TO PREPARE THEM, USE THE PRE-COOKED, VACUUM-PACKED VARIETY INSTEAD.

8 oz. fresh chestnuts or 7 oz. vacuum-packed, cooked, and peeled chestnuts
4 cups vegetable stock (page 8)
¼ cup unsalted butter
1 tablespoon olive oil
8 shallots, finely chopped
1 garlic clove, crushed
1½ cups risotto rice, such as vialone nano, carnaroli, or arborio
⅓ cup white wine
1½ cups freshly grated Parmesan cheese, plus extra to serve
a handful of fresh flat-leaf parsley, coarsely chopped
sea salt and freshly ground black pepper

SERVES 4

If using fresh chestnuts, cut a cross in the blunt end of each one, then put in a roasting pan and cook in a preheated oven at 350°F for 25–30 minutes or until they split open. Let cool, then peel. Coarsely chop the chestnuts.

Put the stock in a saucepan. Heat until almost boiling, then reduce the heat until barely simmering to keep it hot.

Heat the butter and oil in a deep skillet or heavy-bottomed saucepan over a medium heat. Add the shallots and cook for 1–2 minutes, until softened but not browned. Add the garlic.

Add the rice and stir with a wooden spoon until the grains are well coated and glistening, about 1 minute. Pour in the wine and stir until it has been completely absorbed.

Add 1 ladle of hot stock and simmer, stirring until it has been absorbed. Repeat. After about 10 minutes, add the chestnuts and mix well. Continue to add the stock at intervals and cook as before, for a further 8–10 minutes, until the liquid has been absorbed and the rice is tender but still firm (*al dente*).

Add the Parmesan, parsley, salt, and pepper. Mix well. Remove from the heat, cover, and let rest for 2 minutes.

Spoon into warmed bowls and serve with grated Parmesan.

Risotto with Truffles

RISOTTO AL TARTUFO

TRUFFLES ARE SYNONYMOUS WITH ITALY AND ARE A REAL LUXURY. IF YOU ARE LUCKY ENOUGH TO HAVE ONE, SHAVE IT FINELY OVER THE RISOTTO. IF YOU DON'T, AN EXTRA SPOONFUL OF TRUFFLE OIL WILL REMIND YOU OF WHAT YOU'RE MISSING. STORE TRUFFLES IN AN AIRTIGHT JAR OF RISOTTO RICE.

Put the stock in a saucepan. Heat until almost boiling, then reduce the heat until barely simmering to keep it hot.

Heat the butter and oil in a deep skillet or heavy-bottomed saucepan over a medium heat. Add the shallots and cook for 1–2 minutes, until softened but not browned.

Add the rice and stir with a wooden spoon until the grains are well coated and glistening, about 1 minute. Pour in the wine and stir until it has been completely absorbed.

Add 1 ladle of hot stock and simmer, stirring until it has been absorbed. Continue to add the stock at intervals and cook as before, until the liquid has been absorbed and the rice is tender but firm (*al dente*), about 18–20 minutes. Reserve the last ladle of stock.

Add the reserved stock, Parmesan, cream, truffle oil, parsley, salt, and pepper. Mix well. Remove from the heat, cover, and let rest for 2 minutes.

Spoon into warmed bowls and shave paper-thin slices of truffle over the top, if using. Serve immediately.

4 cups vegetable stock (page 8)
¼ cup unsalted butter
1 tablespoon olive oil
8 shallots, finely chopped
1½ cups risotto rice, such as vialone nano, carnaroli, or arborio
⅓ cup white wine
1½ cups freshly grated Parmesan cheese
2 tablespoons light cream
2 tablespoons truffle oil
a handful of fresh flat-leaf parsley, coarsely chopped
sea salt and freshly ground black pepper
1 fresh black or white truffle, to serve (optional)

SERVES 4

Risotto with Lemon and Mint
RISOTTO CON LIMONE E MENTA

MOST COOKS WILL HAVE A COUPLE OF LEMONS IN THE KITCHEN AND MINT GROWING IN THE GARDEN, SO THIS RISOTTO NEEDS LITTLE PLANNING OR FORETHOUGHT. IT'S IDEAL FOR AN IMPROMPTU MEAL WHEN FRIENDS VISIT OR IF YOU WANT A DELICIOUS SUPPER WITHOUT HASSLE.

4 cups vegetable stock (page 8)
¼ cup unsalted butter
1 tablespoon olive oil
8 shallots, finely chopped
1 garlic clove, crushed
1½ cups risotto rice, such as vialone nano, carnaroli, or arborio
⅓ cup white wine
1½ cups freshly grated Parmesan cheese
finely grated zest of 3 lemons
2 tablespoons light cream
a handful of fresh mint, coarsely chopped
sea salt and freshly ground black pepper

TO SERVE:
chopped fresh mint
extra virgin olive oil

SERVES 4

Put the stock in a saucepan. Heat until almost boiling, then reduce the heat until barely simmering to keep it hot.

Heat the butter and oil in a deep skillet or heavy-bottomed saucepan over a medium heat. Add the shallots and cook for 1–2 minutes, until softened but not browned. Add the garlic.

Add the rice and stir with a wooden spoon until the grains are well coated and glistening, about 1 minute. Pour in the wine and stir until it has been completely absorbed.

Add 1 ladle of hot stock and simmer, stirring until it has been absorbed. Continue to add the stock at intervals and cook as before, until the liquid has been absorbed and the rice is tender but firm (*al dente*), about 18–20 minutes.

Add the Parmesan, lemon zest, cream, mint, salt, and pepper. Mix well. Remove from the heat, cover, and let rest for 2 minutes.

Spoon into warmed bowls, top with chopped mint, and drizzle with extra virgin olive oil. Serve immediately.

Risotto with Olives and Red Peppers

RISOTTO CON OLIVE E PEPERONI ROSSI

A ROBUST RISOTTO, RICH WITH MEDITERRANEAN FLAVORS. USE OLIVES THAT HAVE BEEN PITTED AND MARINATED WITH HERBS AND GARLIC, AVAILABLE FROM ITALIAN DELIS. DON'T USE THE CANNED VARIETY. ROASTING PEPPERS CONCENTRATES THEIR FLAVOR BY CARAMELIZING THEIR NATURAL JUICES.

Roast the peppers in a preheated oven at 400°F for 20 minutes, until blistered and charred. Seal in a plastic bag for 10 minutes, then scrape off the skin. Cut the peppers in half and remove and discard the seeds. Cut the flesh into squares. Set aside.

Put the stock in a saucepan. Heat until almost boiling, then reduce the heat until barely simmering to keep it hot.

Heat the butter and oil in a deep skillet or heavy-bottomed saucepan over a medium heat. Add the shallots and cook for 1–2 minutes, until softened but not browned. Add the garlic.

Add the rice and stir with a wooden spoon until the grains are well coated and glistening, about 1 minute. Pour in the wine and stir until it has been completely absorbed.

Add 1 ladle of hot stock and simmer, stirring until it has been absorbed. Continue to add the stock at intervals and cook as before, until the liquid has been absorbed and the rice is tender but still firm (*al dente*), about 18–20 minutes. Reserve the last ladle of stock.

Add the reserved stock and roasted peppers, the Parmesan, olives, parsley, salt, and pepper. Mix well. Remove from the heat, cover, and let rest for 2 minutes.

Spoon into warmed bowls, sprinkle with chopped parsley, and serve immediately.

2 medium red peppers
4 cups vegetable stock (page 8)
¼ cup unsalted butter
1 tablespoon olive oil
8 shallots, finely chopped
2 garlic cloves, crushed
1½ cups risotto rice, such as vialone nano, carnaroli, or arborio
⅓ cup white wine
1½ cups freshly grated Parmesan cheese
⅓ cup black olives, about 10, pitted and coarsely chopped
a handful of fresh flat-leaf parsley, coarsely chopped, plus extra to serve
sea salt and freshly ground black pepper

SERVES 4

Risotto with

Mushrooms, Cognac, and Cream

RISOTTO CON FUNGHI, COGNAC, E PANNA

I LOVE TRADITIONAL ITALIAN FOOD, SO WHEN MY FRIEND INTRODUCED ME TO THIS THOROUGHLY MODERN RISOTTO I WAS PLEASANTLY SURPRISED AT HOW MUCH I LIKED IT. WE ATE THIS RICH, CREAMY RISOTTO AT PECK, A WONDERFUL RESTAURANT IN MILAN. THIS DISH IS VERY SUBSTANTIAL AS WELL AS COMFORTING.

Heat half the butter in a skillet until foaming, then add the mushrooms and cook for 5 minutes. Add salt and pepper. Add the Cognac or brandy, boil until reduced by half, then stir in the cream. Simmer for 5 minutes, until the sauce has thickened slightly. Set aside.

Put the stock in a saucepan. Heat until almost boiling, then reduce the heat until barely simmering to keep it hot.

Heat the remaining butter and the oil in a deep skillet or heavy-bottomed saucepan over a medium heat. Add the shallots and cook for 1–2 minutes, until softened but not browned. Add the garlic and mix well.

Add the rice and stir with a wooden spoon until the grains are well coated and glistening, about 1 minute.

Add 1 ladle of hot stock and simmer, stirring until it has been absorbed. Continue to add the stock at intervals and cook as before, until the liquid has been absorbed and the rice is tender but firm (*al dente*), about 18–20 minutes.

Add the reserved mushroom mixture, the grated Parmesan, parsley, salt, and pepper. Mix well. Remove from the heat, cover, and let rest for 2 minutes.

Spoon into warmed bowls, top with Parmesan shavings, and serve.

½ cup unsalted butter
8 oz. cremini mushrooms, finely sliced
1 tablespoon Cognac or other brandy
3 tablespoons light cream
4 cups vegetable stock (page 8)
1 tablespoon olive oil
8 shallots, finely chopped
2 garlic cloves, crushed
1½ cups risotto rice, such as vialone nano, carnaroli, or arborio
1½ cups freshly grated Parmesan cheese
a handful of fresh flat-leaf parsley, coarsely chopped
sea salt and freshly ground black pepper
shavings of Parmesan cheese, to serve

SERVES 4

Risotto with Seven Wild Herbs

RISOTTO CON SETTE ERBE SELVATICHE

THIS RISOTTO CAME ABOUT BY ACCIDENT. I HAD PICKED SOME WILD HERBS FROM MY GARDEN IN ITALY AND COULDN'T DECIDE WHICH TO USE TO FLAVOR MY RISOTTO, SO I ADDED THEM ALL. THE RESULT WAS FANTASTIC. USE MY SUGGESTION OF HERBS OR CHOOSE YOUR OWN. YOU DON'T EVEN HAVE TO USE SEVEN HERBS, ALTHOUGH IN ITALY THIS NUMBER IS BELIEVED TO BRING GOOD LUCK.

Put the stock in a saucepan. Heat until almost boiling, then reduce the heat until barely simmering to keep it hot.

Heat the butter and oil in a deep skillet or heavy-bottomed saucepan over a medium heat. Add the shallots and cook for 1–2 minutes, until softened but not browned.

Add the rice and stir with a wooden spoon until the grains are well coated and glistening, about 1 minute. Pour in the wine and stir until it has been completely absorbed.

Add 1 ladle of hot stock and simmer, stirring until it has been absorbed. Continue to add the stock at intervals and cook as before, until the liquid has been absorbed and the rice is tender but firm (*al dente*), about 18–20 minutes. Reserve the last ladle of stock.

Add the reserved stock, the Parmesan, cream, mixed herbs, salt, and pepper. Mix well. Remove from the heat, cover, and let rest for 2 minutes.

Spoon into warmed bowls, sprinkle with chopped mixed herbs, and serve immediately.

4 cups vegetable stock (page 8)
¼ cup unsalted butter
1 tablespoon olive oil
8 shallots, finely chopped
1½ cups risotto rice, such as vialone nano, carnaroli, or arborio
⅓ cup white wine
1½ cups freshly grated Parmesan cheese
2 tablespoons light cream
a handful of mixed fresh herbs, such as sage, parsley, basil, thyme, mint, oregano, and marjoram, chopped, plus extra to serve
sea salt and freshly ground black pepper

SERVES 4

Risotto with

Eggplant, Pine Nuts, and Tomatoes

RISOTTO CON MELANZANE, PINOLI, E POMODORI

I FIRST TASTED THIS DISH IN A TINY TRATTORIA IN ROME, ONE BALMY EVENING IN LATE SUMMER. IT ALWAYS REMINDS ME OF BEING IN ITALY. SALTING THE EGGPLANTS BEFORE COOKING WILL REMOVE ANY BITTERNESS AND TOASTING THE PINE NUTS UNTIL GOLDEN WILL INTENSIFY THEIR NUTTY FLAVOR.

1 small eggplant, about 7 oz., diced
3 tablespoons olive oil
4–6 medium Italian plum tomatoes, seeded and chopped
4 cups vegetable stock (page 8)
¼ cup unsalted butter
8 shallots, finely chopped
2 garlic cloves, crushed
1½ cups risotto rice, such as vialone nano, carnaroli, or arborio
½ cup white wine
1½ cups freshly grated Parmesan cheese
⅓ cup pine nuts, pan-toasted
a handful of fresh flat-leaf parsley, coarsely chopped
a handful of fresh basil, coarsely chopped
sea salt and freshly ground black pepper

SERVES 4

Put the eggplant in a colander set over a bowl. Sprinkle with salt and let stand for 10–15 minutes. Rinse to remove the salt and pat dry. Heat 2 tablespoons of the oil in a skillet, add the eggplant, and cook until golden. Add the tomatoes and cook until softened.

Put the stock in a saucepan. Heat until almost boiling, then reduce the heat until barely simmering to keep it hot.

Heat the butter and remaining oil in a deep skillet or heavy-bottomed saucepan over a medium heat. Add the shallots and cook for 1–2 minutes, until softened but not browned. Add the garlic.

Add the rice and stir with a wooden spoon until the grains are well coated and glistening, about 1 minute. Pour in the wine and stir until it has been completely absorbed.

Add 1 ladle of hot stock and simmer, stirring until it has been absorbed. Continue to add the stock at intervals and cook as before, until the liquid has been absorbed and the rice is tender but firm (al dente), about 18–20 minutes. Reserve the last ladle of stock.

Add the reserved stock, the eggplant and tomato mixture, the Parmesan, pine nuts, parsley, basil, salt, and pepper. Mix well. Remove from the heat, cover, and let rest for 2 minutes.

Spoon into warmed bowls and serve immediately.

Artichoke Risotto

RISOTTO CON I CARCIOFI

TRY TO BUY YOUNG ARTICHOKES WITH LONG, UNCUT STEMS. THE SHORTER THE STEM, THE

TOUGHER THE ARTICHOKE TENDS TO BE. YOUNG ARTICHOKES ARE ALSO LESS FIBROUS. FIRMLY

CLOSED ARTICHOKES ARE AN INDICATION OF FRESHNESS; IF THE LEAVES ARE OPEN THEY ARE OLD.

To prepare the artichokes, pull off the tough outer leaves and cut off the spiky, pointed top. Remove the stalk and cut each artichoke lengthwise into 4 segments if small or 8 segments if large. Cut away the fuzzy, prickly choke. Squeeze the lemon over the segments to prevent discoloration. Set aside.

Put the stock in a saucepan. Heat until almost boiling, then reduce the heat until barely simmering to keep it hot.

Heat the butter and oil in a deep skillet or heavy-bottomed saucepan over a medium heat. Add the shallots and cook for 1–2 minutes, until softened but not browned. Add the garlic and artichoke segments and cook for 2–3 minutes.

Add the rice and stir with a wooden spoon until the grains are well coated and glistening, about 1 minute. Pour in the wine and stir until it has been completely absorbed.

Add 1 ladle of hot stock and simmer, stirring until it has been absorbed. Continue to add the stock at intervals and cook as before, until the liquid has been absorbed and the rice is tender but firm (*al dente*), about 18–20 minutes.

Add the Parmesan, mascarpone, parsley, salt, and pepper. Mix well. Remove from the heat, cover, and let rest for 2 minutes.

Spoon into warmed bowls and serve with grated Parmesan.

4 small or 2 large globe artichokes
1 lemon, halved
4 cups vegetable stock (page 8)
¼ cup unsalted butter
1 tablespoon olive oil
8 shallots, finely chopped
1 garlic clove, crushed
1½ cups risotto rice, such as vialone nano, carnaroli, or arborio
⅓ cup white wine
1½ cups freshly grated Parmesan cheese, plus extra to serve
2 tablespoons mascarpone cheese
a handful of fresh flat-leaf parsley, coarsely chopped
sea salt and freshly ground black pepper

SERVES 4

Broccoli and Lemon Risotto
RISOTTO CON BROCCOLETTI E LIMONE

I WAS SERVED THIS RISOTTO IN SANT' AMBROGIO—A RESTAURANT NAMED
AFTER THE PATRON SAINT OF MILAN. PURPLE SPROUTING BROCCOLI HAS A
DELICIOUS NUTTY FLAVOR, BUT IF YOU CAN'T FIND IT USE BROCCOLINI INSTEAD.

4 cups vegetable stock (page 8)
¼ cup unsalted butter
1 tablespoon olive oil
8 shallots, finely chopped
2 garlic cloves, crushed
1½ cups risotto rice, such as vialone nano,
  carnaroli, or arborio
½ cup white wine
2½ cups broccoli rabe, cut into 1½-inch
  lengths, or broccoli florets
1½ cups freshly grated Parmesan cheese
finely grated zest of 2 lemons
a handful of fresh flat-leaf parsley,
  coarsely chopped, plus extra to serve
sea salt and freshly ground black pepper

SERVES 4

Put the stock in a saucepan. Heat until almost boiling, then reduce
the heat until barely simmering to keep it hot.

Heat the butter and oil in a deep skillet or heavy-bottomed
saucepan over a medium heat. Add the shallots and cook for
1–2 minutes, until softened but not browned. Add the garlic.

Add the rice and stir with a wooden spoon until the grains are well
coated and glistening, about 1 minute. Pour in the wine and stir
until it has been completely absorbed.

Add 1 ladle of hot stock and simmer, stirring until it has been
absorbed. Repeat. After 10 minutes, add the broccoli. Continue
to add the stock at intervals and cook as before, for 8–10 minutes
longer, until the liquid has been absorbed and the broccoli and
rice are tender but still firm (*al dente*).

Add the Parmesan, lemon zest, parsley, salt, and pepper. Mix well.
Remove from the heat, cover, and let rest for 2 minutes.

Spoon into warmed bowls, sprinkle with chopped parsley, and
serve immediately.

index

conversion charts

Weights and measures have been rounded up
or down slightly to make measuring easier.

VOLUME EQUIVALENTS:

American	Metric	Imperial
1 teaspoon	5 ml	
1 tablespoon	15 ml	
¼ cup	60 ml	2 fl.oz.
⅓ cup	75 ml	2½ fl.oz.
½ cup	125 ml	4 fl.oz.
⅔ cup	150 ml	5 fl.oz. (¼ pint)
¾ cup	175 ml	6 fl.oz.
1 cup	250 ml	8 fl.oz.

WEIGHT EQUIVALENTS:

Imperial	Metric
1 oz.	25 g
2 oz.	50 g
3 oz.	75 g
4 oz.	125 g
5 oz.	150 g
6 oz.	175 g
7 oz.	200 g
8 oz. (½ lb.)	250 g
9 oz.	275 g
10 oz.	300 g
11 oz.	325 g
12 oz.	375 g
13 oz.	400 g
14 oz.	425 g
15 oz.	475 g
16 oz. (1 lb.)	500 g
2 lb.	1 kg

MEASUREMENTS:

Inches	Cm
¼ inch	5 mm
½ inch	1 cm
¾ inch	1.5 cm
1 inch	2.5 cm
2 inches	5 cm
3 inches	7 cm
4 inches	10 cm
5 inches	12 cm
6 inches	15 cm
7 inches	18 cm
8 inches	20 cm
9 inches	23 cm
10 inches	25 cm
11 inches	28 cm
12 inches	30 cm

OVEN TEMPERATURES:

110°C	(225°F)	Gas ¼
120°C	(250°F)	Gas ½
140°C	(275°F)	Gas 1
150°C	(300°F)	Gas 2
160°C	(325°F)	Gas 3
180°C	(350°F)	Gas 4
190°C	(375°F)	Gas 5
200°C	(400°F)	Gas 6
220°C	(425°F)	Gas 7
230°C	(450°F)	Gas 8
240°C	(475°F)	Gas 9